MW01171660

KINESIOLOGY
Common Sense
Volume I

Myung Chill Kim

KINESIOLOGY

Common Sense

Volume I

Published by Myung Chill Kim

Copyright © 2022

Library of Congress Control Number: 2021925492

$9.95

About the Author

Myung Chill Kim was born in Korea in 1942. He is the seventh child in a family of eleven brothers and sisters and has lived with Martial Arts and Oriental Medicine his entire life. He is the 37th generation Doctor of Oriental Medicine in his family.

Master Kim participated in the Vietnam War as a Korean Tiger Trooper and as a Tae Kwon Do and close combat instructor.

He moved to the United States in 1970. Master Kim's first book, *Acupuncture for Self-Defense*, was published a year later in 1971. *Oriental Medicine and Cancer*, was published in 1996. *Chi Gong: Medicine from God* was published in 1999. *Tae Kwon Do (Kwang Moo Ryu)* was published in 2006. *Kinesiology: Common Sense* was published in 2022.

Master Kim performed acupuncture anesthesia in June of 1973 at the Naval Hospital at Portsmouth, Virginia. This was the first time in American medical history where anesthesia acupuncture was performed.

Master Kim worked at the Trans- Alaska Pipeline System as a security officer, at the New York City Department of Ports and Terminals as an Inspector, and as Criminal Investigator at the Bronx.

Master Kim attended New York City Technical College for three years in the '80s to study Western science.
Kim graduated from the Emperor's College of Oriental Medicine in 1984 and received his degree of Doctor of Oriental Medicine in 1988 from Samra University of Oriental Medicine.

Currently, Master Kim practices acupuncture, herbal medicine, Chi Gong and Martial arts in Oklahoma City, Oklahoma.

For more information and best practices of Master Kim, please visit:

www.myungchillkim.com

www.kwangmooryu.com

Dedication

This book is dedicated to my grandfather who passed away in the mountain of Northeastern part of Korean peninsula as a resistance army Captain against Japanese invaders. I also dedicate this book to my father, older brothers and the North Korean Nal Pa Lam martial art masters who taught me martial arts.

Acknowledgments

My thanks also go to Master Chen Yo Yu for his Chinese calligraphy.

For demonstrating poses in photos, I would like to thanks to Keith Zeff and Roger Blacius. Many thanks to Ralph Penland for helping with photo editing and big thanks to Steve Eagleston who helped proofread this book.

Also, thanks to Hester Anne Brown for editing.

Finally, I would like to thank my wife Sung and my children John and Stella, and family members for their continued support.

Warning - Disclaimer

This book is intended to provide information on the general theory of kinesiology based on Martial Art techniques and should only be used as a general guide.

If there are any mental or physical limitations on completing any of these movements, one should consult with a medical physician first prior to attempting the instructed movements in this book.

This book is not for obtaining information or for breaking sports rules and regulations, especially for Baseball and Softball pitching, Tennis ball serving, Javelin throwing techniques, Discus and Shot Put.

Myung Chill Kim and Seven Galaxy Publications shall have neither liability nor responsibility to any person or organization with respect to any mental or physical damage caused directly or indirectly by the information in this book.

The New York City Police Department
Police Academy

On recommendation of its faculty and by virtue of the authority
vested in it by the Police Commissioner has awarded to

MYUNG CHILL KIM

this certificate as evidence of the satisfactory completion of

PEACE OFFICER COURSE

Given in the City and State of New York
in the month of   JULY   nineteen hundred and 83

Robert J. L. Grace
POLICE COMMISSIONER

Daniel F. Flynn
COMMANDING OFFICER, POLICE ACADEMY

9

Kinesiology

운동요법

(Oon Dohng Yo Buhp)

Table Of Contents

Preface

Standing and walking homo sapiens (early modern humans) appeared on earth nearly 2 million years ago. The first humans began to use hands and tools for farming, built houses, hunted animals, and were skilled at warfare.

Except for a few martial arts experts in India, China, and Korea, the first humans did not know how to use tools properly. Using tools with the correct kinesiology not only prevents injuries, but also helps the body with "energy efficiency". Using correct kinesiology will foster productivity. For example, if one uses a computer mouse and feels numbness on the hand, then try moving the hand to the center of the keyboard. Another option is to replace using a mouse at a desktop with a laptop touch pad. You will feel much better at once.

The 20th century was the age of globalization. The 21st century will be space travel age. Please read this book before migrating to another planet.

Introduction
"Bruce Lee's 1-Inch Fist Punch"

Fig. 1-1   **Fig. 1-2**

Fig. 1-3

Fig. 1-1: Close the target with right hand.
Fig. 1-2: Lift up right foot.
Fig. 1-3: Stomp with right foot, pivot, then turn the waist and punch at the same time stretch left hand backward

Fig. 1-4   **Fig. 1-5**

Fig. 1-4: Tae Kwon Do and Karate ready pose.
Fig. 1-5: Punch with rear hand and do not turn the waist.

Fig. 1-6   **Fig. 1-7**

Fig. 1-6: Boxing ready pose.
Fig. 1-7: Punch with rear hand and pivot with rear foot.

Fig. 1-8   Fig. 1-9

Fig. 1-8: Shaolin style ready pose.
Fig. 1-9: Palm strike with rear hands, pivot rear foot at the same time stretch front hand backwards.

Bruce Lee took boxing lessons and learned Wing Chun Kung Fu. Wing Chun style Kung Fu emphasizes "on hand" techniques more than kicking. His entire life was dedicated to martial arts. Bruce Lee's one-inch punch was very powerful, because he pivoted his foot and turned the hip and waist. I wish I would have suggested to Bruce Lee that he should stomp the front foot and stretch the other hand in the opposite direction of the dominant punch.

Any "in-shape" martial artist can achieve the unique "Wing Chun Kung Fu" style technique within six months. A boxer can train using the

"Wing Chun Kung Fu" technique better than a Karate or Tae Kwon Do expert.

Joe Lewis was an American kickboxer, point karate fighter, and actor. Lewis was also a Karate instructor, but Lewis' punch was not strong enough because Lewis did not turn his waist to create torque power.

While growing up in Hong Kong, Bruce Lee learned how to box in the ring. However, he may not have been able to win in any weight division in boxing as Lee's fans may think. He was a just a dedicated martial artist and an extraordinarily talented movie actor.

Demonstration of Internal Power: Master Yim's Pushing Hand

Fig. 1-10

Fig. 1-11

Here is another demonstration of Internal Power by Korean martial art Master Yim.

Watch the demonstration on Korean TV program "Body God (나는 몸신이다)" ep. 25 (at 28-minute mark), as referred to in Figs. 1-10 and 1-11.

Master Yim slightly hit the punching bag with his palm (Fig. 1-10). Ten people were pushed away and fell on the floor (Fig. 1-11). Master Yim practiced internal style martial art for the last 50 years.

The internal style emphasizes practicing meditation and secret breathing exercises like Chi Gong and Tai Chi. Internal style of martial arts cannot be explained or applied with Newton's laws of motion.

In contrast to Internal stylists, External stylists cannot reach the highest goal of the tremendous Power of Chi.

You can study internal style by reading my other book *Chi Gong: Medicine from God (3rd Edition)*, currently available on Amazon.com.

Kinesiology of Stomping

There are seven hand techniques to increase power in my Kwang Moo Ryu style Tae Kwon Do book. Compare with ordinary Tae Kwon Do, Karate, and kick boxing. Stomping is one component out of the seven hand techniques. The above techniques are for **simultaneous stomping cases**.

If one keeps performing labor work such as regular shoveling, axing, or hammering continuously, then use **sequential stomping** techniques.

You can face both situations, if you must dig up a trench faster in short period time or dig a trench slowly to take up more time. To dig up a trench fast in a short period of time, apply the **simultaneous stomping** technique and to dig a trench slowly to take up more time, apply **the sequential stomping technique**.

All these techniques not only increase better performances of athletes, but these techniques also prevent injuries. All the above theories are derived from the theory of "we were four legged animals two million years ago". Please refer to and read the "Crawling" section towards the end of this book.

Below are descriptions of the "Simultaneous Stomping" technique and the "Sequential Stomping" technique. These differing techniques help you transfer maximum energy to the tool you are using to get the job done more easily.

Simultaneous Stomping Technique

Simultaneous Stomping is very useful when fighting in close combat with either a staff, spear, lance, sword, or bayonet. I have created martial art forms that use stomping and employ left and right sides of the body equally.

Raise the tool and raise the foot closest to the target. Bring the tool down while dropping the foot. Time the leg and hand movements so that the foot stomps and the tool strikes at the same time.

A-Type Sequential Stomping technique:

Raise the tool and raise the front foot, the one closest to the target as above. Then shift your body weight as you stomp the front foot. Stomp with REAR foot at the same time strike with tool.

Manual workers will generally prefer Sequential Stomping because sequential stomping gives greater endurance and power, although the duration of a job that may take several hours. A worker can get the most power from B-type Sequential Stomping. You can increase power by raising the tool and foot higher, stomping harder, and hitting the ground both the feet and tool in rapid, sequential succession.

For better endurance during sequential stomping, use a normal, continuous pace, raise tool and foot with less distance from the ground, and stomp gently, as if you are taking a gentle step.

While working in mud or sand, it is best to put down a hard board or metal sheet to stomp on. While working with farm implements, machinery, axe, or pickaxes, you can use Sequential Stomping techniques to strengthen body movements while either pushing, pulling, turning, or striking.

In doing routine manual work, use both sides of the body. To avoid unbalanced muscle and skeletal structural issues, switch hands when using tools. For example, if you are right-handed and frequently use the right side, switch sides, and use the left side of the body.

Similarly, when using stomping techniques, alternate the foot position every fifteen minutes. This practice will gain strength, flexibility, and coordination on both sides of the body. At that point, you will learn to use less effort and the job will go by much easier.

A place where you can see the effectiveness of stomping is at festivals and parades that feature giant Chinese dragons. Underneath the dragon is a team of dancers using hoists with poles to keep the creature slithering continually. The power of walking and stepping gives the dancers strength and endurance to manage the weight of the Chinese dragon costumes.

Guide For Wearing Wrist Weights During Sports

One-handed sports including tennis, the javelin throw, shot put, discus throw, and bowling should allow weights to be on the other side of the wrist. Wrist weights will help develop a better-balanced body during sports and will help to prevent injuries. I hope that each sports organization would permit wrist weights during sports.

I strongly suggest that wrist weights are allowed and recommended the following wrist weights for use opposite of the dominant hand:

a. Police baton: 8 oz.
b. Tennis Racket: 9 to 11 ounces
c. Javelin: 1.3 to 1.8 Lbs.
d. Shot Put: 12 to 16 Lbs.
e. Discus: 2.2 to 4.4 Lbs.
f. Hand grenade: 2 Lbs.
g. Bowling ball: 14 to 18 Lbs.
h. Meat Cleaver or Butcher's knife (1 to 1.6 Lbs.)
i. Honing knife (average 10 oz.) Try to use the same weight of cleaver and honing knife

1.Shoveling

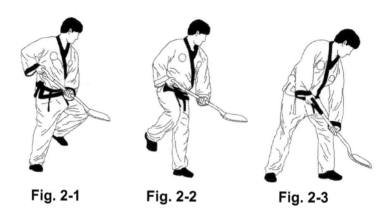

Fig. 2-1   Fig. 2-2   Fig. 2-3

First, lift the front foot, then rear foot, and then stomp the foot as you shovel at the same time.

You can stomp with only the front foot when you are in hurry. Stomping the front and rear foot gives more power and it is good for steady work during long hours.

The more you stomp harder, naturally stomping harder makes the arm movement harder too, like when you are in a battlefield and digging a trench.

2.Sledge Hammering

Fig. 2-4   Fig. 2-5

Fig. 2-6

First, lift front foot, rear foot, and stomp at the same time while hammering.

3.Axing

Fig. 2-7

Fig. 2-8

Ordinary Axing

Fig. 2-9   Fig. 2-10

Fig. 2-11   Fig. 2-12

Fig. 2-9 through Fig. 2-12: Sequential Stomping

Fig. 2-13

Fig. 2-14

Ordinary Axing

30

Fig. 2-15

Fig. 2-16

Fig. 2-17

Fig. 2-18

Fig. 2-15 through Fig. 2-18 – Sequential Stomping

4.How to Lift Patient Easily

1. Stomp with left foot (patient's head side). At the same time slide the patient to the left. (Simultaneous stomping) (slide only) *For lightweight patient*

2. Stomp with right and then left foot, at the same time slide the patient to the left. (sequential stomping) (slide only) *For average weight patient*
   * If you want to lift the patient: after right and left foot stomping, lift up the patient (sequential stomping)

3. Stomp with left, right and then left foot, at the same time slide the patient to the left. (sequential stomping) (slide only) *for heavyweight patient*

   "How to lift patient" video at
   https://youtube.com/@kwangmooryu

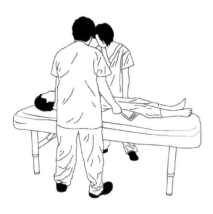

5.Lifting a Box

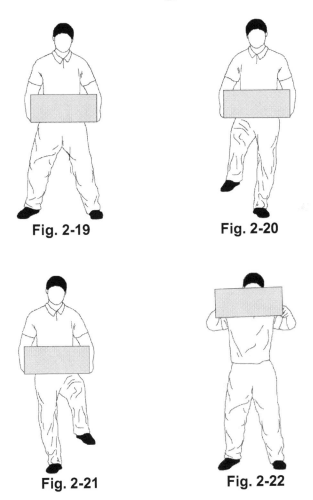

Fig. 2-19   Fig. 2-20

Fig. 2-21   Fig. 2-22

Pick up the box from the ground to the conveyer or storage rack. lift the box up from waistline to the chest, first step right and left foot and then place it.

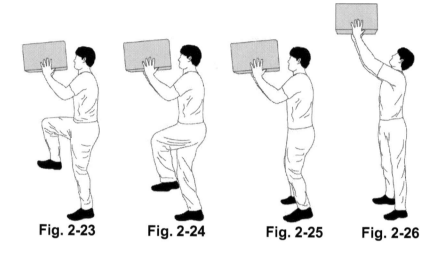

Fig. 2-23   Fig. 2-24   Fig. 2-25   Fig. 2-26

Lift the box from chest to the above the head, first step right and left foot and then place it. For box weights less than 50 pounds, use "Sequential Stomping" with a gentler foot impact – step, instead of stomp. Stomping transfers more power from the body to the box when you stomp quickly or forcefully. Be careful to avoid knee or back injury.

6.Opening a Jar

Fig. 2-27

Fig. 2-28

Fig. 2-29

Fig. 2-30

The right hand is used for closing, and the left hand is used for opening a jar. When closing the jar, stomp with left foot. When opening the jar, stomp with the right foot. For left-handed persons, do the opposite.

A senior citizen's health and strength can be checked by looking at how the senior uses the power of the hand to grab and open a pickle jar.

One should train to use both hands from an early childhood age to open and close a jar to prevent unnecessary injury to wrist, thumb joint and/or muscles.

7.Pulling Out a Tooth

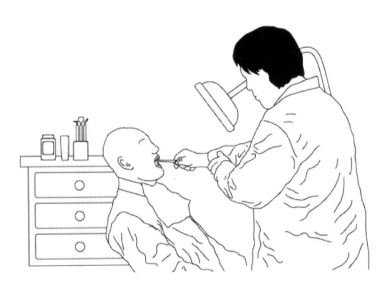

Fig. 2-31

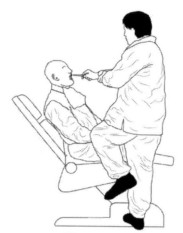

Fig. 2-32

Fig. 2-33

38

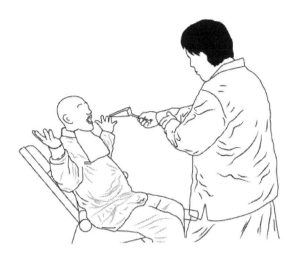

Fig. 2-34

When pulling the tooth, stomp with the front foot first, and then stomp with rear foot second at the same time pull the tooth.

When pulling the tooth out of the client's mouth in the direction towards your body and the desired extraction angle.

8. Cleaver/Butcher's Knife (with Meat)

Fig. 2-35

This illustration is of a man holding meat with no chance to practice with the left hand. The repetition of cutting for many years causes body imbalance, joint and muscular pain.

Cleaver/Butcher's Knife (without Meat)

Fig. 2-36

The man is practicing cutting without any meat using up and down exchange with both hands to balance out muscles and joints evenly on both sides of his body. If you are right-handed, practice cutting meat with the left hand and exchange the position of the knife.

Fig. 2-37

Practice cutting without meat while stomping, too. Right hand up, left knee up. When you chop down, right hand goes down and left foot stomps.

These days, we have electric saw to cut meat with. We don't need to cut meat in this position, but this is a good way to exercise.

Fig. 2-38

This illustration depicts the man using both a butcher knife and a honing knife to practice cutting without stomping.

Fig. 2-39

It is better to practice using stomping techniques while alternating honing and butcher knives in each hand.

43

Refer to free demonstration video
https://youtube.com/@kwangmooryu

If you cut hard meat or bone, you may use an electric saw. If you are not cutting, then use the non-knife holding hand sometimes to hold meat. If a chef is cutting tough meat or bone with the cleaver, the chef may cut the item much faster with shorter movements while the other hand holds the food.

Although hard meat and bone can be chopped with one hand, you can also practice cutting side to side from left to right, or from right to left, or even using thrusting motions to cut meat by slicing in a forward direction or downwards backward direction.

Keep in mind to use alternate arms. During resting time, you can practice cutting and chopping movements to balance the hand arm coordination.

The following movements should be practiced during non-cutting time for a few minutes every hour.

Cutting with a Honing Knife

If you cut tough meat or bone with more force, then stomp with the opposite foot. When you are using a meat cleaver with a honing knife, move the other hand in the opposite direction (up or down).

For example, use the right hand to cut while stomping with the left foot, and use the left hand to cut while stomping with the right foot.

MARTIAL ARTS

Fig. 2-40

45

Karate kata is a type of martial art that uses form-pattern. "Jut Te" has this movement.

A 40-year-old butcher visited from Texas to my clinic in Oklahoma City. The butcher drove 300 miles to see me because he could not move his right hand. It appeared to be injured due to repetitive motions used while cut meat for over twenty years.

The butcher was planning to sell the business, even though it was successful. Although he was a dedicated Karate black belt, he did not know how to apply Karate Kata to daily work, nor did he know how to fight. I told the butcher that most of Martial art masters and instructors did not know how to properly apply Karate Kata or how to fight. The butcher was able to use techniques learned in kinesiology sessions with me to apply the proper technique of how to cut meat.

Fig. 2-41   Fig. 2-42

My Kwang Moo Ryu Tae Kwon Do form
#16 has up and down palm with
stomping.

Downward palm with stomping is good for
breaking technique, but originally was
designed for hitting down on the enemy's
head or body. Using palm causes internal
injury and is very dangerous. For more
information, please purchase my Tae Kwon
Do book on amazon.com and purchase my
videos from www.kwangmooryu.com.

Fig. 2-43

This is TKD form from my Form 16.

Fig. 2-44   **Fig. 2-45**

The martial artist is using higher fists with
one simultaneous stomp to break the
cement block.

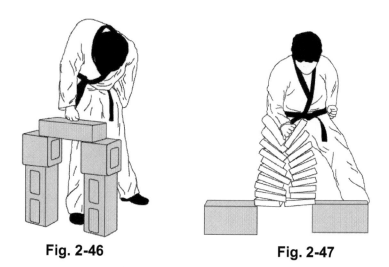

Fig. 2-46   **Fig. 2-47**

Fig. 2-46 and Fig. 2-47 are the worst examples of kinesiology because this shows how to break the hand easily. Most martial artist breaking technique is like this, do not know how to apply the Kata (Form) movement, it is a good example of the how to break the hand. Even some martial art textbooks showed this movement.

A man claimed to be an 8th degree black belt in a Tae Kwon Do organization. The man did not know about the correct martial art forms or kinesiology. Some martial art historians said that the 20th century is "The Dark Age of Martial Art".

9.Post Office

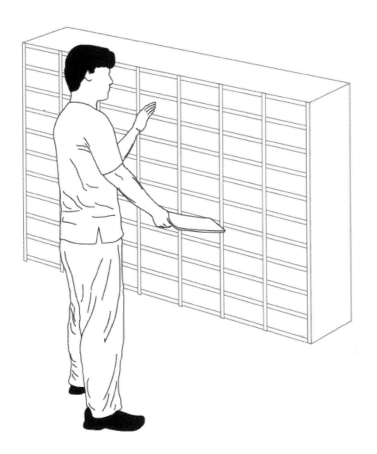

Fig. 2-48

51

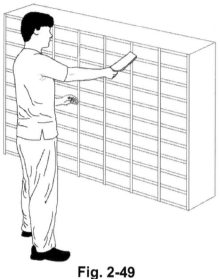

Fig. 2-49

A postal worker who learned Tai Chi as a moving meditation threw at least 2000 envelopes to many different zip codes in multiple directions per day.

The postal worker complained of arm, shoulder, and scapular area joint pain. He used the same arm to throw letters for 15 years. Amazingly, he practiced Tai Chi every day, yet did not know how to apply the movements at work or in self-defense. He developed severe pain, so I advised him to use the other hand at the same time in the opposite direction.

I also found out that he practices Tai Chi every morning with 24 movements. I told him that the first movement of these Tai Chi movements are exactly fit the letter throwing movements. He said that he was taught that Tai Chi was moving meditation. So, he did not know how to apply it in daily work.

Fig. 2-50

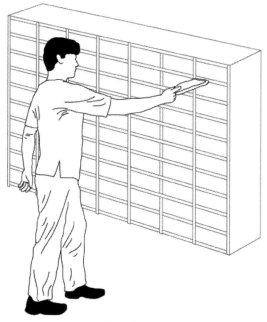

Fig. 2-51

Some letters are heavy then use other side of foot with mild stomping.

MARTIAL ART

Fig. 2-52   Fig. 2-53

I give a few examples of Tai Chi movements in my Tae Kwon Do book. Boxing does not allow back hand or fist strike because it is too fast and if apply it waist movement, too dangerous. Tai Chi allows for back hand and fist strikes. One of the Tai Chi movements uses the back hand. Praying mantis technique is very fast and uses a lot of back hand strikes. Praying mantis is the fastest movement in martial arts.

The first movement of Tai Chi is called "Brush wild horse's mane". This movement is relaxing with soft feel. I think this movement is moving meditation with deep slow breathing and it is a character of internal style martial art.

10.   Handling Books in a Library

Fig. 2-54 Bookshelves in Library

Fig. 2-55   **Fig. 2-56**

Repeated one hand motions could damage wrist.

Fig. 2-57   **Fig. 2-58**

Using other hand up and down opposite direction of the book.

Fig. 2-59   **Fig. 2-60**

Hold another book with the other hand
and move the opposite direction while
use either a book (as pictured in Fig. 2-
59 and Fig. 2- 60) or a wrist weight (Fig.
2-61 and Fig. 2- 62) in the other hand.
The wrist weight should be no more
than one pound.

Fig. 2-61   **Fig. 2-62**

All workers, athletes and martial artists work
with hands. The use of repetitive movement of
hands for years can cause not only wrist,

elbow, and arm problems, but also may affect the neck, shoulders, and scapula.

Sports coaches and martial artist masters advise tennis players to handle a racquet with one hand. However, it is advised for the tennis player to practice with the opposite hand (the non-playing hand) at home.

Practicing with the opposite hand is also advised for construction workers. I had treated a 65-year-old, retired construction worker who had "tilted right scapula" problem, severe pain at the scapula area, and bicep and triceps muscles. He was also a carpenter and used a hammer with one hand for over 40 years. I asked the construction worker whether anyone advised the construction worker to exercise the opposite of the body (the non- dominant side). He stated that no one recommended him to work using the other side of the body (the non-dominant side).

The construction worker was exhausted from using the same side of the body. He always went home too tired to do anything more.

11. Fire Rescue

Fig. 2-63   Fig. 2-64

Front foot stomp **(Fig. 2-63 and Fig. 2-64)**

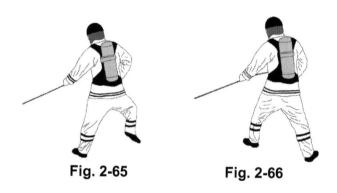

Fig. 2-65   Fig. 2-66

Rear foot stomp **(Fig. 2-65 and Fig. 2-66)**

When rescuing people from a burning building, cliff, or water, first stomp with the front foot then the rear foot in sequence while pulling.

Fig. 2-67   **Fig. 2-68**

Rescued people should set the rope
on top of one foot, then press the
other foot on top of the rope.

12. Cowboy

Fig. 2-69

Fig. 2-70

Stomp with the front foot first, and then stomp with rear foot at the same time pulling the cow.

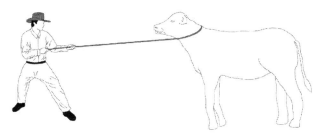

Fig. 2-71

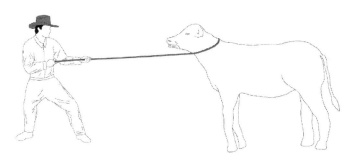

Fig. 2-72

63

13. Pushing a Car

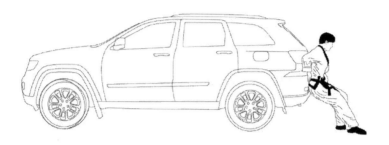

Fig. 2-73

Incorrect **position** – pushing with back

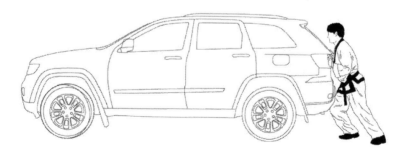

Fig. 2-74

Ordinary pushing forward

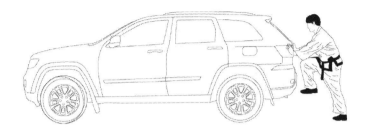

Fig. 2-75

Correct position: Push with stomp preset

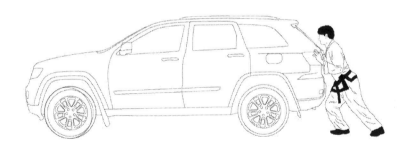

Fig. 2-76

Pushing with stomp will give more power.

65

Fig. 2-77   **Fig. 2-78**

Fig. 2-77: Push the car or any heavy material with vertical palm as in Tai Chi movement. This movement is good for pushing with Chi energy.

Fig. 2-78: Shows the man pushing with horizontal palm will give more physical force. Better muscular coordination.

14. Baseball Pitching

Ordinary Pitching

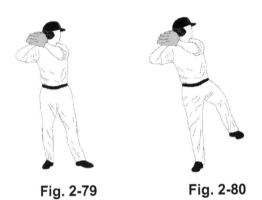

Fig. 2-79   Fig. 2-80

Fig. 2-81

Better Method

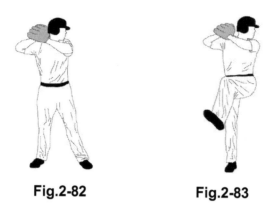

Fig.2-82   Fig.2-83

Fig. 2-84

Better Method - lift left foot and stomp while pushing the left hand outwards outstretched behind the body.

Fig. 2-85

Fig. 2-86

Fig. 2-87

Fig. 2-88

From looking at **Fig. 2-85**, use left foot to step into position at **Fig. 2-87**.

Fig. 2-89

Figures 2-85, 2-86, 2-87, 2-88, and **2-89** shows the ordinary way of pitching baseball. The pitcher throws a ball with the right hand and leaves the left hand holding the glove at the waist. This ordinary method is not the correct way to pitch baseball.

A turning waist is the main power source when pitching baseball. One should try to stomp with the left foot (or dominant foot).

This is the usual body mechanic scene in baseball pitching. However, the pitcher should try to throw a ball while pushing the opposite glove hand towards the back side, as seen in Kung Fu Weapon practice. Such body mechanics may add speed, power, and accuracy.

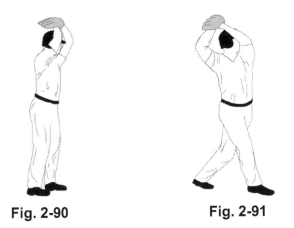

Fig. 2-90   Fig. 2-91

Fig. 2-91 shows the man stepping with right foot.

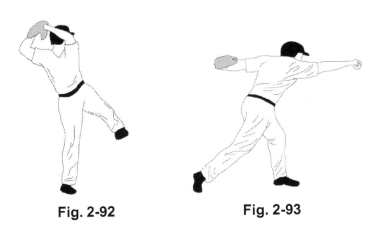

Fig. 2-92   Fig. 2-93

Fig. 2-92 shows the man stomping with left foot, and **Fig. 2-93** shows the man stretching left hand backwards at the same time while the left foot had stomped.

Fig. 2-94   **Fig. 2-95**

Fig. 2-96

Fig. 2-94, 2-95, and **2-96** depict a man in
baseball who is kneeling to throw the ball
in the normal style (no good).

72

Fig. 2-97   Fig. 2-98

Fig. 2-99

Fig. 2-97 depicts the baseball player who
is starting with both hands close together.
The player throws the ball while turning
the body and stretching the left hand
behind his body. This is the correct way to
throw a baseball in the kneeling position.

Fig. 2-100

Fig. 2-101

Fig. 2-102

Figs. 2-100, 2-101, and 2-102 shows the baseball player catching and throwing.

Fig. 2-103

Fig. 2-104

Fig. 2-105

Fig. 2-103 shows a player catching the ball.

Fig. 2-104 shows the player twisting the body with both hands together, while the bending the knees.

Fig. 2-105 shows the pitcher ready to throw the ball with two hands coming towards each other. This is the better method.

75

Fig. 2-106

Fig. 2-107

Fig. 2-106 shows the pitcher throwing the ball with two hands together in parallel.

Fig. 2-107 shows demonstration of swinging two hands together, kicking the left foot out and slapping the ground with left palm simultaneously.

This is the best way to throw a ball when on the ground.

15. Baseball Batting

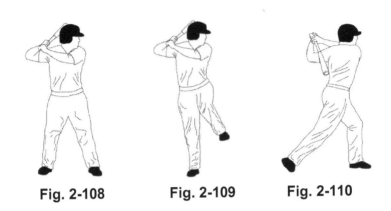

Fig. 2-108   Fig. 2-109   Fig. 2-110

Figs. 2-108 and 2-109 depict a man applying a stomp to prevent injuries to elbow joint.

Baseball batting is akin to hitting a tree. The impact comes back onto the wrist, elbow, and shoulder.

The better method is stomping to create less pain on the joint. Stomp while turning the waist as to reduce the impact of elbow pain and risk of injury.

Stomping provides more force to the impact on the ball during batting to provide a greater distance upon hitting the ball than with ordinary batting.

16. Softball Pitching

Ordinary pitching

Fig. 2-111

Fig. 2-112

Fig. 2-113

Better Method

Fig. 2-114

Fig. 2-115

Fig. 2-116

Fig. 2-117

Stomp with left foot and throw and stretch out left hand. This is better than ordinary.

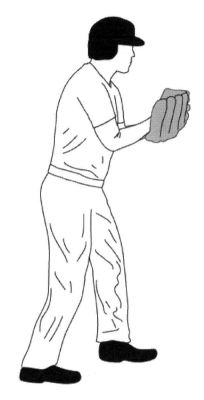

Fig. 2-118

Right foot

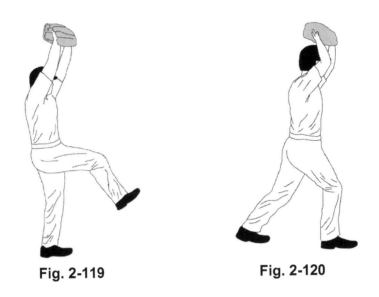

Fig. 2-119   **Fig. 2-120**

Figs. 2-118, 2-119, and 2-120 depict a pitcher about to pitch a ball. Start with lifting hands up with right foot stepping.

Fig. 2-121

Fig. 2-122

Figs. 2-121 and 2-122 depict the pitcher stomping with left foot and stretching left hand backward.

17. Football Throwing

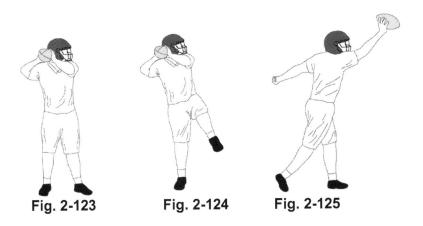

Fig. 2-123   Fig. 2-124   Fig. 2-125

Fig. 2-123 depicts ready position, palms gripping ball.

Fig. 2-124 and Fig. 2-125 depict the player stomping with the left foot while throwing the ball with the right hand and simultaneously thrusting left hand backwards

18. Throwing a Basketball

Fig. 2-126

Fig. 2-127

Ordinary throwing

Fig. 2-128

Fig. 2-129

Stomping with left Foot is better than Ordinary, but not perfect.

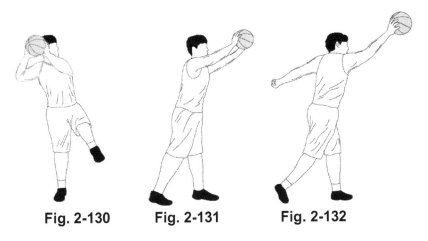

Fig. 2-130   Fig. 2-131   Fig. 2-132

Figs. 2-130, 2-131, and 2-132 show the player throwing a basketball. Start with both hands on the same side of the body, lift the left foot and reach forward with both hands on the ball, turn and stomp to create more momentum while thrusting the left hand behind the body.

Fig. 2-133   Fig. 2-134   Fig. 2-135

Figs. 2-133, 2-134, and 2-135 depict a short distance stomp.

19. Tennis

A. Ordinary Method

Fig. 2-136   Fig. 2-137

B.

Fig. 2-138   Fig. 2-139

Figs. 2-138 and 2-139 depict a stomp while the left hand moves backwards behind the body, which is better than Ordinary, but not perfect.

C.

Fig. 2-140

Fig. 2-141

Figs. 2-140 and 2-141 depict a player starting with both hands on the same side, while turning the waist and stomping to create more momentum.

Figs. 2-140 and 2-141 are better than **Figs. 2-138 and 2-139.**

D.   Tennis with Wrist Weight

Fig. 2-142   **Fig. 2-143**   **Fig. 2-144**

A Tennis racket is 9-to 11 ounces. If you are
holding the tennis racket with one hand,
then you would need a weight that is of equal
weight of the racket on the opposite wrist,
as well for optimized momentum and for less
potential damage to the body.

20. Golf

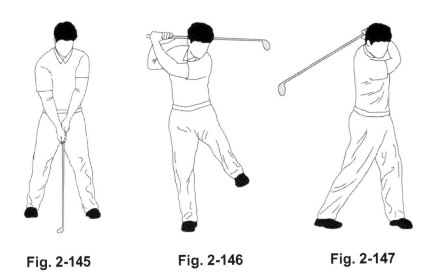

Fig. 2-145   Fig. 2-146   Fig. 2-147

Stomping will give you much more force, but you can lose accuracy.

You will need much more practice for it to be effective.

21.Frisbee

A.

Fig. 2-148 **Fig. 2-149**

Ordinary position

B.

Fig. 2-150 **Fig. 2-151**

Cross hands; left hand throw and left foot stomp.

C.

Fig. 2-152

Fig. 2-153

Fig. 2-154

Fig. 2-155

Hold frisbee with left hand, stomp with right foot and turn body inward.

D.

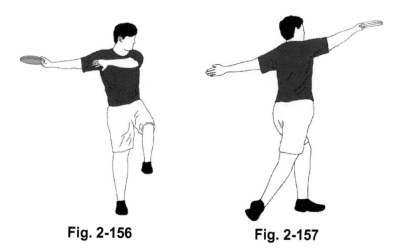

Fig. 2-156   Fig. 2-157

Hold frisbee with right hand, while stomping
with the left foot and turning the body inward.

22. Javelin

A.

Fig. 2-158    Fig. 2-159

Normal position

B.

Fig. 2-160   Fig. 2-161

Use two hands together on the same side
while stomping.

B. (continued)

Fig. 2-162

Fig. 2-162 depicts turning with twist in the waist after stomping to create more momentum. Stretch out left hand backwards for accuracy.

C. Javelin with Wrist Weight

Fig. 2-163

Fig. 2-164

Practice using wrist weights with the javelin to balance the body both sides equally.

23. Discus Throw

A.

Fig. 2-165   Fig. 2-166   Fig. 2-167

Ordinary position; shows the man stretching out with both hands in the opposite direction. This will slow down body spin.

B.

Fig. 2-168   Fig. 2-169   Fig. 2-170

Start with both hands in same side, turn and stomp to create more momentum. Close the body with both hands like figure skater to turn body faster. Stomp with left foot and twist the waist to throw with right hand while stretching out left hand backwards.

C. Discus with Wrist Weights

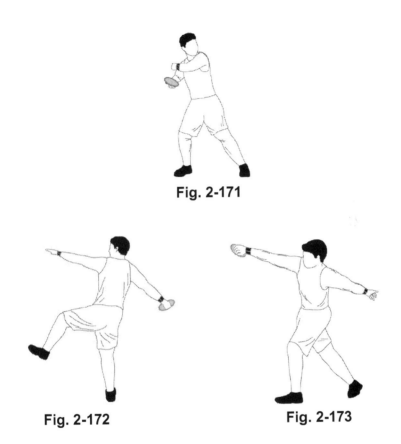

Fig. 2-171

Fig. 2-172

Fig. 2-173

Use wrist weights to balance the body to minimize joint and muscle pain.

24. Shot Put

A. Ordinary

Fig. 2-174   Fig. 2-175   Fig. 2-176

In Ordinary, one hand is stretched out and other hand is down by the side.

B. Better Method

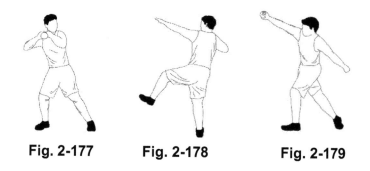

Fig. 2-177   Fig. 2-178   Fig. 2-179

Start with both hands in same side, turn and stomp to create more momentum. Also close the body with both hands as like figure skating to turn body faster.

C.   Shot Put with Wrist Weights

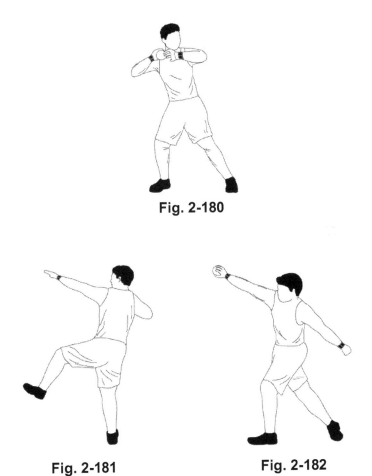

Fig. 2-180

Fig. 2-181   Fig. 2-182

Modify the wrist weight from one-fifth to one-tenth of the weight of the shot put.

25. Bowling

Fig. 2-183   Fig. 2-184

Fig. 2-185

Do not use stomp as you may lose accuracy.
If using wrist weight on the other wrist as
same weight of the bowling ball but its weight
is 12 to 18 Lbs. It should be modified to one
fifth or one tenth of the weight of these balls.

26. Judo

Fig. 2-186

Fig. 2-187

Fig. 2-188

It requires speed but try stomp too. stomping power diminished by the mat but street fight situation, ground in hard in most of the times.

27. Hand Grenade

A. Ordinary

Fig. 2-189   Fig. 2-190

B. Better Method

Fig. 2-191   Fig. 2-192

Start with both hands in same side, turn and stomp and turn the waist to create more momentum.

C. Wrist Weight

Fig. 2-193

Fig. 2-194

Softball Throw Style
(Hand Grenade Throw with Softball Style)

A. Ordinary

Fig. 2-195   Fig. 2-196   Fig. 2-197

Right hand makes an arch backwards.

B. Better Method

Fig. 2-198   Fig. 2-199   Fig. 2-200

Start with both hands in same side, turn and stomp to create more momentum. The right hand makes an arch. Left hand stretches backwards.

C. Wrist Weight

Fig. 2-201

Fig. 2-202

Fig. 2-203

Start with both hands in same side, while wearing wrist weights, turn and stomp to create more momentum. The right hand makes an arch.

Kneel and Throw (Hand Grenade)

A. Ordinary

Fig. 2-204

Fig. 2-205

B. Better Method

Fig. 2-206

Fig. 2-207

Start with both hands in same side. Turn and throw while stretching left hand backwards.

C. Wrist Weight

Fig. 2-208

Fig. 2-209

107

Throwing Hand Grenade While Lying Down

A. Ordinary

Fig. 2-210   Fig. 2-211

B. Better Method

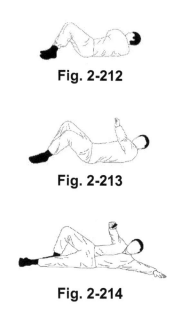

Fig. 2-212

Fig. 2-213

Fig. 2-214

Figs. 2-212, 2-213, and 2-214 show hands close together while turning waist and throwing the grenade. Kick, slide with left foot and slam left palm to the ground.

C. Throwing grenade with wrist weights

Fig. 2-215

Fig. 2-216

Fig. 2-217

28. Police Baton Overhead Strike

A. Better Method

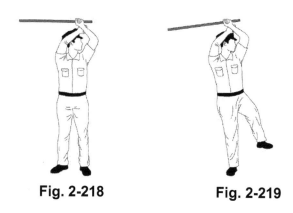

Fig. 2-218   **Fig. 2-219**

Fig. 2-220

Overhead strike/other hand push the wrist
and stomp.

B. Wrist Weight

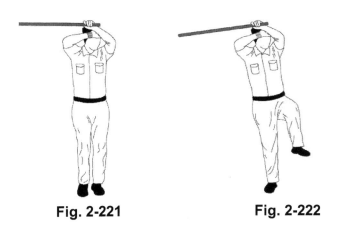

Fig. 2-221   Fig. 2-222

Fig. 2-223

Police Baton (Side Strike)

A.

Fig. 2-224

Fig. 2-225

Strike Sideways while other hand pushes the wrist and stomp.

B. Wrist Weights

Fig. 2-226

Fig. 2-227

Police Baton Thrust

A. Better Method

Fig. 2-228   Fig. 2-229

Thrust-other hand push the wrist and stomp.

B. Wrist weight

Fig. 2-230   Fig. 2-231

29. Knife Throwing

A. Ordinary

Fig. 2-232

Fig. 2-233

B. Better Method

Fig. 2-234

Fig. 2-235

Start with both hands in same side, turn and stomp to create more momentum. Hold handle while throwing knife.

C. Wrist Weight

Fig. 2-236

Fig. 2-237

Dagger Throwing

A. Ordinary

Fig. 2-238   Fig. 2-239

B. Better Method

Fig. 2-240   Fig. 2-241

Start with both hands on same side. Turn and stomp to create more momentum.

Dagger is heavier. Hold blade while throwing.

C. Wrist weight

Fig. 2-242

Fig. 2-243

30. Axe Throwing

A. Ordinary

Fig. 2-244

Fig. 2-245

B. Better Method

Fig. 2-246

Fig. 2-247

Start with both hands in same side, turn and stomp to create more momentum while stretching left hand backwards.

C. Wrist weight

Fig. 2-248

Fig. 2-249

31. Lance

Fig. 2-250

Fig. 2-251

The modern training lance is named the *kwan do* (*guan do*) after a famous third century Chinese General Guan Yu or Kwan Yu (Died A.D. 220). He is said to have fought with a 100-pound lance.
Today's training lance weighs about 30 pounds.

If you are training with the *kwan do* and have any difficulty with the weight, use the B-Type Sequential Stomping technique. If you participate in reenacting historic battles, sometimes you might not be able to find a lightweight weapon to use in mock combat. Then you need to know the stomping techniques to deal with a heavier weapon.

32. German Sword

Fig. 2-252

Fig. 2-253

A high school student learned German sword fighting, but the instructor did not teach him basics. The student ended up with shoulder surgery. It is important to learn the proper form and basic stomping techniques.

33. Pistol

Fig. 2-254 police style

Fig. 2-255 military style

Fig. 2-256

Fig. 2-257

Martial art weapon maneuvering style - arm muscle will be less tired and create more accuracy.

Pistol with wrist weights

Fig. 2-258

Fig. 2-259

34. Bayonet Skill

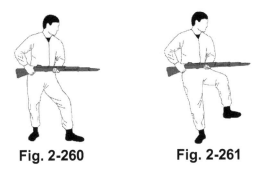

Fig. 2-260   **Fig. 2-261**

Pick up the bayonet and stomp.

Fig. 2-262 Thrust with stomp   **Fig. 2-263**

Pull bayonet backwards while lifting the knee.

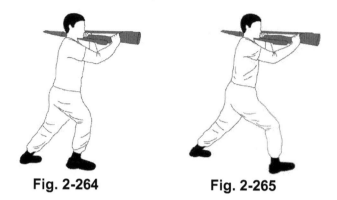

Fig. 2-264   **Fig. 2-265**

Butt Stroke Upward and Thrust

Fig. 2-264 depicts the butt of the bayonet thrust upward direction striking upwards.

Fig. 2-265 depicts the butt of the bayonet pushed forwards. This is a simultaneous movement in sequence with strong force. Thrust up, thrust forward.

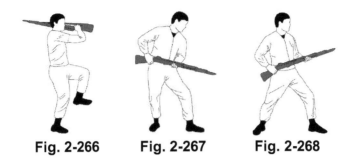

Fig. 2-266   Fig. 2-267   Fig. 2-268

Fig. 2-266 shows the stomp while lifting the butt of the bayonet to prepare for the front of the bayonet to cut down the opponent (**Fig. 2-267**). **Fig. 2-268** is the original position.

Fig. 2-269   Fig. 2-270

Figs. 2-269 and 2-270 depict bayonet sparring training with a wooden staff using a soft towel. This is not correct. Since bayonet fighting uses both sides of the body, place soft towels on both ends of the staff.

Work-Related Injuries

People come to America to either work as an employee or choose to be self-employed. "Multicultural America" contains different countries and ethnic groups. The average white American is taller and larger than the average Asian person. If one chooses to work at an American factory, there are machinery, tools, and equipment too large and heavy for the average Asian person to handle.

One Asian female patient complained to me that she developed carpal tunnel syndrome in the wrists along with shooting arm pain. The pain was so sharp that she could not continue working at the grocery store. I quickly realized after hearing her concerns that the cash register stand at her job was way too high for her.

The same Asian female patient described how the American white store owner at her job was tall enough to put a bag on the counter and fill the bag with groceries. However, when my patient tried to complete the same tasks as the American store owner, she found the goods she was assigned to complete as part of her daily tasks were all higher than her shoulder-level.

I suggested that she instead build and place a 20-inch (W) x 1-ft (H) x 4-ft (L) wooden stool on the floor. This solution would have greatly reduced the stress and strain on her wrists and shoulders since the countertop was too high for her without the stool.

Similarly, I had another patient who was a Korean cook who complained about the same carpal tunnel syndrome and severe arm pain as described above. I found out that they worked daily at one restaurant plus worked part-time at another restaurant. The Korean cook was 5' 3" tall. I advised him to build the same wooden stepping stool and to carry it to any kitchen where he cooked so that he could easily work on the kitchen countertops without strain.

Architecture Hazards

I traveled to over thirty states across America and went to over fifteen different countries. I have observed many beautiful steep roofs as beautiful as one could imagine in a fairy tale.

I have observed beautiful steep roofs in many regions that take on very heavy snow and rainfall. When I moved to Boston, Massachusetts in 1990, there were many cities and town hall buildings with steep roofs. The Boston-style architecture reminded me of old European-style castles with cone-shape roofs commonly found in Switzerland and Germany. The historical Boston architecture was so beautiful yet practical, because the roof styles avoided any caving in of the heavy snowfall, rainwater, and ice into the building. The steep roofs with gutters are very practical to avoid roof sagging or holes.

When I toured the Boston area, I saw one ice skating rink building with very low-angle roof, close to a flat roof style. I had predicted that the roof would collapse with heavy snow fall and rain someday. My prediction was right-- the roof collapsed a few years later when there was extremely heavy snowfall!

"When you go to Rome, do as Romans do!"

The phrase was used to encourage all to observe Roman laws. In modern times, people use the phrase to follow local customs.

When I traveled to Caribbean countries, local restaurants offered dishes that were very salty. I understood that people who work in tropical climates sweat a lot.

Since I do not do any more strenuous exercise to sweat much, nor participate in any excessive activities, I added less salt to my meals to balance out the fact that I was a tourist in a tropical region who was there for a short time – maybe one week.

- We will produce thirty-three professionally made kinesiology videos soon.

  Please visit **www.kwangmooryu.com** to sign up for updates.

- I will give permission for Royalty free printing of this book to any Country's GDP below $6,000 per year, except for Countries that speak the following languages: English, Spanish, Italian, Russian, French, Arabic and Chinese, because I may be entering a publishing contract to distribute my book in those languages.

I like to encourage to translate this book with their own language and distribute it free or very low price by the government. Contact me via email *info@myungchillkim.com* to fill out an application.

I. Breathing Exercise

Fig. I-a: Inhale through nose for 5 seconds.

Fig. I-b: Exhale for 10 seconds. Motion
hands as if you are breaststroke
swimming.

Fig. I-c: Inhale for 5 seconds. Motion hands as if you are breaststroke swimming.

Fig. I-d: Exhale for 10 seconds. Gradually increase inhale and exhale to 1:2 ratio.

II. Breathing Exercise

Fig. II-a: Have both palms facing sky. Inhale 5 seconds.

Fig. II-b (right): Bend upper body sideways while one hand is over head and other hand touches the waist. Exhale 10 seconds. Increase it to 1:2 ratio.

Fig. II-c (left): Bend upper body sideways in opposite direction.

Fig. II-d: Do it as in *Fig. II-a*. Gradually increase inhale and exhale with 1:2 ratio.

III. Stretching While Lying Down

Fig. III-a: Lie down on your back and stretch in an isometric exercise. First, inhale through nose for 5 seconds, and then exhale for 10 seconds through mouth. Hold breath for 10 seconds. Complete ten sets of this exercise two times per day.

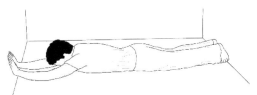

Fig. III-b: Lie down on your stomach and push hands and feet to both directions.

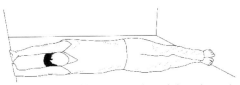

Fig. III- c: Lie down sideways and push hands and feet to both directions.

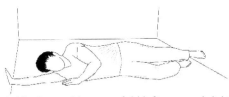

Fig. III-d: Lie down sideways, fold left arm and right leg and push right hand and left foot outwards in both directions. Repeat this process with other side.

IV. Isometric for Hands and Feet

Fig. IV

Western style isometric exercise is only for specific parts of the muscle (i.e., hands or feet). But Asian isometric exercises are for both hands and feet together. Inhale small amount of air through nose in 2 seconds, send air down to the diaphragm and hold breathing for 10 seconds while extending all fingers and bend all toes upward. Exhale through the mouth slowly and relax all tensed muscles. Repeat it 10 times per set. 2 or 3 sets per day. Isometric exercise – develop only designated muscle group only.

Isotonic exercise- build up lung, heart, and other muscle groups as our daily exercise, such as running, swimming, and weightlifting.

V. Bottles

Fig. V-a

The bottle above contains 70 % blood mixture with fluid. Compare this figure to a standing man in the upright position. Blood circulation reaches the brain and blood flowing from the leg to the heart is very difficult.

For example, rub above the outer side calf and ankle area with a small wooden stick, and you will feel pain. This pain indicates that everyone has blood stagnation related issues in the leg.

People with back, hip, and joint related issues as well as diabetics will feel more pain on one side of the body. Massage the outer areas of both legs every day with either a stick or hands.

Fig. V-b

The bottle above depicts the same 70 % blood and fluid mixture. It is positioned sideways like a four- legged animal.

This example shows how the human blood circulates throughout the body to the heart to head, and from heart to leg, showing the even distribution of blood in the veins around calf muscles, heart muscles, and head.

Fig. V-c

This figure depicts a bottle using the same 70 % blood and fluid mixture distribution, showing a man standing upside down like a yoga pose.

This upside-down position, showing the smooth blood distribution from the calf muscles, heart, and head is a good position for younger folks. However, this position is not good for older folks with high blood pressure or high eye pressure, because the risk can be very damaging to the body.

VI. Raising Both Feet Against a Wall

Fig. VI-a

Lie on your back and raise up both feet against wall. This position is good for facial wrinkles, Parkinson's, Alzheimer's disease, and thyroid issues. While lying down, you can massage your face and neck. In my over seventy-five years of practice, I have seen lots of problems. My hypotheses are as follows:

Taller people with Norwegian, Finnish, Swedish (Scandinavian countries) are more susceptible to varicose veins, and blood and lymph fluids are not able to reach the brain and upper part of the body easily. Therefore, taller people are more susceptible to lymphoma and cancer.

Shorter people, such as the French, are not necessarily susceptible to the same group of diseases as taller people.
Usually, shorter people live longer than taller people.

Robots stand up in position like human, so robot's head part lubrication oil is pull downward compared to lower part.

Also, the robot's lower part of the robot body bears more pressure from upper part of the robot's body, so the robot needs more adjustment of bolts and nuts.

When the robot is not in use for long periods of time (resting position), the robot should be imitating the Figure VI-a) movement, raising the up feet up against the wall like a human.

Stomping techniques should be applied to robots, too.
When the robot pulls, pushes, or lift, the robot needs extra power to save energy.

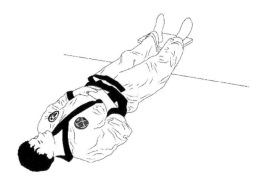

Fig. VI-b

Lie on your back and raise up both feet
against the chair. People with high blood
and/or eye pressure should to this movement
for about five minutes a few times a day.

VII. Crawling

Fig. VII-a

Bear crawl with palms and bottom of feet.

Fig. VII-b

Crawl like an infant by using palms and knees for older people.

149

The Benefits of Crawling

The first humans who walked with 2 legs
on this earth around 1.8 million years ago.
Anthropologists have said that due to
gravitational forces pulling down on the
human body, the skeletal structures of
human beings have evolved since the first
homo-erectus. The human skull has
gotten bigger due to brain development,
and the pelvic bones have shrunken,
while cervical vertebrae and neck appear
weaker in modern times compared to our
ancient ancestors.

This information is commonly known amongst
doctors of Oriental medicine. Our upper body
has better blood circulation than the lower
part of the body because the lower part of the
body has poor circulation due to the
gravitational pressure from the upper body.
Note the common occurrence of varicose
veins in women.

When there is an injury in the hand or arm,
the injury heals faster than injuries to the leg.
If one's foot is amputated, sometimes the
infection does not heal, and the doctor cuts
off more of the leg. This is true, not only for
diabetics, but also healthy, young people.

How can one prevent these circulation problems?

A wise person crawls for at least ten minutes per day, with both palms and soles of the feet touching the ground. Kneepads and gloves are optional.

The bear crawl, as seen in **Fig. VII-a**, is more efficient for circulation and overall health than the infant crawl, as depicted in **Fig.VII-b**. You can use palms and knees, like the infant crawler, but the infant crawl is much less effective than the bear crawl.

However, elderly people cannot perform the bear crawl, so infant crawl is recommended if the elderly do not have any knee problems.

Crawling stimulates internal organs. Both the bear crawl and the infant crawl will adjust alignment of the spine as well as develop muscles in the hands and feet, arms and legs, and the hips and shoulders, while distributing weight proportionately.

Some exercises that work for the balancing of the upper and lower part of the body are Swimming, yoga, Pilates, and of course, crawling.

Crawling is a good exercise as a warm up or limbering up before and after any sports activities, especially before and after running.

The weakest part of our human body is the neck. For example, when one watches a movie at the front row seat in a theater, he or she will most certainly experience neck pain. If crawling every day is implemented into the daily routine, then one will suffer less with neck pain whiplash after experiencing a car accident.

We have rehabilitation hospitals and medical research teams at research universities who would be wise to study the human benefits of either the bear crawl or the infant crawl. Anyone who tries crawling for one week will experience positive benefits to their overall health.

Crawling is one of the martial artists' secrets. Both the Shaolin monks and Taoist followers crawl every day at a minimum for one hour to maintain health and longevity. All athletes would be wiser to incorporate crawling into their training techniques. In addition to breaking world records, crawling would enable athletes to keep their winning records.

Even the famous gold medalist Olympians Michael Phelps (Swimming) and Usain Bolt (100 m running) should crawl!

A doctor of sports medicine said the 1970's was for running. The 1980's were the era of jogging, in the 1990's walking became vogue. The 21st century and beyond is for crawling!

Runner's Syndrome

Many devoted runners and joggers complain about pain in the leg muscles, hips, knee, and or ankle joints, as well as blurry eyes, vertigo, and migraines. All these syndromes are well-known in Western sports medicine.

Due to running and jogging, females may have ovarian pain, prolapse, as well other pain in the uterus and on the sides of the breasts. The female runner might even experience endometriosis, or even ovarian cancer or uterine problems, as well as breast tumors and/or breast cancer.

Athletes and runners who have not shown any spinal injuries or any surgical scars are considered "in perfect condition and health" when passing standards and tests used by Western physicians.

The healthy athletes appear to have lean bodies, with no severe illnesses and no prior accidents in their medical history. From the point of view of Oriental Medicine, a very different standard and opinion is rendered concerning many vigorous sports.

My oriental medicine practice has studied the effects of running, jogging, jumping and any related sports activities that affect the hip joints. My study is part of The Gall Bladder Acupuncture Channel #30 ("GB #30") points located on both sides of the hip joint. GB #30 studies in my oriental medicine studies have found that sports activities that affect the hip joint leads to problems in the body, which must be carefully maintained and administered to in specific ways with treatment.

I am the only Oriental medicine doctor in the world who studied GB #30 points pertaining to sports activities. My research spans over fifty years. Here is what I found.

Female athletes are adversely affected at GB #30 hip joints, because of the larger and wider hip structure than that of the male hip structure. The female hip and related pelvic joints are looser during menstruation, thus overwhelming the body during such strenuous sports activities.

The Gall Bladder Acupuncture Channel begins on the lateral side of the eyes and circles twice around the head area (on each side of the head), moves downward to the top of the shoulders, the sides of the breasts,

155

sides of the hips, sides of the legs, sides of the ankle and ends at the fourth toe.

The Gall Bladder Acupuncture Channel are energy meridians interconnected throughout both sides of the body. Challenge yourself and those you know to run less Bear crawl or infant crawl every day, starting with one minute per day and eventually distribute time evenly between walking and crawling.

For more information on my theories that no one else has ever discovered or written, please read my other book, *Oriental Medicine and Cancer (Revised Edition)*.

VIII. Kegel Exercise with Soft Ball

Chi Gong, Yoga or Kegel exercise

Fig. VIII-a

First inhale a little air thru nose hold it and squeeze anus muscle lightly for 5 second and then exhale thru mouth for 5 seconds.

Fig. VIII-b

Repeat this exercise the same way as described above in **Fig. VIII-a**, but this time, try holding and squeezing a small, soft ball in each hand to make the exercise more fun and enjoyable.

Complete this exercise while squeezing the anus muscle and/or for females, the vaginal wall muscles, and anus muscle together. This exercise is for anyone. Use a small, soft ball, a child's toy soft ball, not a stress ball. Using balls helps make one more motivated to perform this exercise.

Taking Off Shoes at Home

You **must** take off shoes in your home.

Americans contract more lung cancer than Asians, even though Americans smoke less than Koreans or other Asians. Also, sanitation and medical facilities are much better than in Asian countries and pollution control is better than in most of the third world countries.

I have observed the American lifestyle for the last 50 years from the point of view of medical anthropology.

What is big difference between East and West? Koreans, Japanese and Indians take off their shoes at home. But most Americans wear shoes in the house.

When Americans come home from work, they usually take a shower or wash their hands. They also use air purifier, humidifiers, heaters and air conditioners to control the air quality of the room.

Furthermore, they wash and disinfect mattresses and pillows for allergens. But germs are spread all over the floor from shoes that were worn all day and went many different places.

Even if one vacuums the carpet a couple of times per week, it does not disinfect the carpet. If an infant plays or crawls around the floor, the baby could contact germs that dropped from the shoes of the family and guests.

Also, almost every house- hold has one, two or even three pet animals. Do they keep them clean and in a sanitized condition?

Korean and Japanese used to keep dog at outdoor and cat in indoor.

Most Asians, especially Koreans and Japanese, dry their bodies and feet thoroughly after taking a shower. Most Caucasian Americans do not dry their body and feet enough with a towel and then step on the bathroom floor. The mat gets wet and usually they do not wash it and leave it there for few days. It will produce many germs as in a germ incubator in a medical lab.

For another example, if an electrician or cable T.V. repairman goes into the home, there can be more than ten different types of animal feces from the ground that can be tracked inside. This can even affect toddlers who pick up a cracker from the floor.

A physician may allow a patient to wear shoes while lying down on the exam table. Germs can be transmitted easily to the body because it is close to the wounds, mouth and nose. Americans even sit on a bed while wearing shoes or sometimes lie down with shoes on too.

How about wash your hand and clean your shoes? When an electrician or cable television repairman visits your house, give them disposable shoe covers to wear temporarily while at your home.

IX. How to Treat Coronavirus Through the Use of Natural Methods

"SWEAT IT OUT"

To adequately treat infections a basic understanding of how the body works to rid itself of harmful organisms is important. During the germ infection, having a fever is not a bad thing; it is our body's natural defense mechanism kicking in to fight against harmful bacteria, viruses, and other invading organisms. Modern scientific research reveals that germs (bacteria and viruses) are only able to live in our body when the body is at a normal temperature level.

The traditional Korean method of healing the body against bacterial or viral infections is through elevating the body temperature during the beginning of an infection.

It does not have to be a respiratory organ infection only, even you can apply it to any infection such as tonsillitis, infected wounds with mild fever, etc.

When you catch a cold or flu (bacteria and virus), first check the body temperature. (97-degree F/36.1 C- normal).It is advised that the person heat up the room. This can be done by using a portable electric heater and humidifier.

Prior to the procedure you may take a hot shower or bath. Then cover your face and entire body with a long beach towel and /or wear hooded sweatshirt and socks. Cover your entire body with two blankets. Place one stick on each side of the armpits to make breathing easier – for example, make a tent for breathing when you have a towel over the face.

The sticks should be one inch in diameter (2.5 cm) and 20 inches (50 cm) long or longer for bigger person. Then you will sweat it out for an hour. This process can be safely repeated for two or three days until symptom have improved. Your body temperature will go up to 2- degree F/ 1.1 degree C after an hour of sweating.

For this to be affective you must start at the first sign of symptoms; when you start feeling like you are coming down with the common cold, a scratchy throat but virus infection symptoms are mild fever (98.6-degree F/ 37 C), chills, ache, fatigue, cough, and headache.

For example, then you must sweat it out immediately and not wait. You may feel much better, repeat it next day but keep in mind that even if you feel better this does not mean it is completely gone.

You need to this process for two or three more days until the yellow or green phlegm color is white which means the infection is gone.

Who can and cannot use this method?

Do not start this procedure when you start coughing up phlegm, vomiting, shortness of breath, chest pain and have high fever (over 101 degree / 38.3 C to 106-degree F/ 41.1 degree C). You must go to emergency room or seek for urgent medical care.

One can do this procedure in a private sauna as well. Wear a hooded sweatshirt, trousers, and socks. Heat the room temperature to150 degrees F (66 degree C). Do this for 30 minutes.

After sweating it out, one should drink enough water to prevent dehydration.

When a person has been infected by the Coronavirus, the first three days of symptoms are usually very mild. During this time the amount of the virus is at its lowest level in the body, therefore sweating it out at the beginning is the best method to rid the body of the virus.

I have been treating hundreds of patients with sweat it out method for common cold and flu symptoms in Boston MA for twenty years and ten years in Oklahoma City, Oklahoma.

There have been many individuals and families in the Oklahoma City area who got better through using the sweat it out method during the initial stage of their corona virus infection. Doing it sooner the best thing; they were able to sweat it out. They did not suffer symptoms at all in the most of cases.

Last June, a mother whose son was thirty years old and who is naturopathic doctor with a practice in Colorado informed me that her son had used this method.

He became infected by coronavirus and using his sauna was able to sweat it out and able to rid himself of the virus through this. He did not get this information from me. I am guessing that he obtained this information of sweating it out from another source.

This method may apply to any infectious disease, infection of the eye, ears, throat infections such as tonsillitis and sinus infections. It can be used in infections on the internal organs provided there is no high fever (over 100-degree F.) You can apply this method to any type of infectious disease and be able to see results.

We are in the age of uncertainty of what kind of virus will be spread and developed. The vaccine may not work well or mutate as often as the influenza virus. The time is now, and until we need a permanent solution to cure coronavirus, "sweat it out". If there is no cure for coronavirus, then Western medical practitioners might potentially resort to experimenting on coronavirus with mice, cats, dogs, monkeys, and humans in a medical trial by using elevated body temperature method.

We knew that germs live in our body temperature level. We can get rid of it by elevate body temperature. Is it possible to cooling down our body below our normal body temperature level to get rid of it? I guessed and imagined it for long time. I found out that very young infants, the elderly cannot reach high fevers during a germ- related or viral infection, because their bodies are weak. Their body temperatures are unable to elevate to a fever level. The physical response of infants and elderly bodies appear to cool down instead of raising to a fever level.

I have not confirmed this theory on lower body temperatures of infants and the elderly from Western medical science yet. If anyone researches the correlation of lower body temperatures, then potentially the coronavirus or germ can be would like to suggest that any scientist should research on this subject.

I have treated many Covid patients who have had coughing, headache, loss of sense and smell, permanent lung damage, heart issues, liver issues, and gallbladder issues. I helped these people successfully except few senior citizens who are over 80 years old.

Korean Culture

About 2,000 years ago, Korea had much more vast land territories than present day. Primitive Korea not only included the modern-day Korean peninsula, but also included Manchuria (modern day China), Siberia (modern day Russia), and the south-eastern part of Mongolia. Primitive Korea was always cold during the winter season. The weather was usually below 40 degrees Fahrenheit or Celsius. Koreans developed warmth by warming up the floor system of a house.

Koreans also built a small sauna near the house. A sauna was usually built for a community of Koreans, not individually owned. This tradition carried through generations until around 1970, after the Korean Health Department banned a small sauna due to sanitation problems.

About seventy-three years ago, I followed my mother to an all-women's only sauna. Only women's saunas existed to help with related female-only medical issues.

When I was about 6 years old in the year 1948, there was a small and old warehouse building that was the local women's sauna. One side of the building had a small, but long half-cylinder-shaped room. The entrance looked like an Eskimo igloo. People got into room only by crawling. The room was very dark inside and a little dim light from burning wood was there. I waited outside beside the sauna for about an hour. Most of the middle and senior-aged women wore dirty, old clothes and even covered their entire bodies with straw sacks. The women tied their hair with filthy rag towels.

The scene was very grotesque, as if I was looking at a group of beggars. The women looked very scary and primitive, as if they were cavewomen.

A few female customers came out in irregular intervals with sweaty bodies and nasty body odors. There was no bath or shower facility in the sauna. I told my mother that I would never come back to that nasty, filthy place again!

I believe that the Korean sauna culture was handed down through The Bering Strait, Alaska, then into North and South America.

"The Mongol Spot" - When a baby is born, the baby's hip shows about a palm sized coloring. The coloring, resembling a bruise, appears to look like a spot, or streak, and appears for about year among Korean, Manchurian, Mongol, Japanese, Tibetan and Native Americans.

Native Americans like to decorate their hats with bird feathers. Native Americans conducted a ritualistic sky burial to honor the dead and feed the birds. The sky burial is like what the Koreans did, where the dead were placed on a wooden rack, and the body was eaten by birds. Koreans did sky burial over 3,000 years ago. After that, Koreans were influenced by Chinese culture and buried the dead underground. The sky burial custom remains in Tibet today, where the dead bodies are cut in a ritual setting and thrown to the birds to eat.

Historical American Medicine Traditions

Bleeding has been a main treatment in traditional American medicine. The American President George Washington contracted a flu-like virus. Washington's physician bled about two quarts (or around two liters) of the President's blood. Eventually, Washington died from anemia, along with other complications. Bleeding methods were very popular in historical American medicine until about 1900, when the practice of bleeding was banned by the US. Government.

Perhaps President Washington would have been able to live longer if he had "sweat it out", like the Native Americans. Historically, Native Americans were seen as "savages" and prejudiced against. The culture of "sweat it out" has not been accepted in modern American medicine traditions.

In 2020, which is about 220 years from the President Washington historical era, I sent letters to many government officials with information regarding the coronavirus. The letters I mailed contained the signatures of over thirty people who survived. The survivors all "sweat out" the coronavirus and were grateful to have known of this Korean traditional medicine.

Eastern culture and Western culture

When I arrived to America in 1970, I saw an evangelist on TV criticize meditation as "a hippie's demonic ceremony".

Meditate on what? Meditate on not thinking. Meditate on clear thought. Meditation is not familiar with American culture. Over fifty years has passed. Meditation, or Zen meditation, is practiced everywhere - in Yoga class, Martial arts schools, psychiatrist offices, and even at some Christian churches.

In my Kinesiology book, Americans can easily and clearly understand all the illustrations with instructions.

My Chi Gong book describes the invisible power of Chi energy. Chi energy is not tangible, so some people can feel chi energy, and some people cannot feel chi energy; other people interpret chi energy as a false claim. Many people can only understand worldly phenomena through tangible senses only. "Seeing is Believing".

Acupuncture treatment is popular among Americans. More than thirty-five percent of Americans have been treated with Acupuncture. Acupuncture theory is based on following the Acupuncture Chi energy channels. Western nerve system is tangible and visible, but Acupuncture channels are invisible.

173

Martial Arts in America

The most participated sport in America is neither baseball, basketball or football. Asian martial arts are the most "participated in" popular sport in America. Americans understand punches, kicks, grappling, and throwing well. However, many Americans struggle to interpret pattern forms such as Kata.

For correct martial arts forms and patterns, check out my Kinesiology book and other books on Amazon.com.
Kinesiology videos are on www.kwangmooryu.com with examples of correct and incorrect form interpretations.

Since most Americans perceive form patterns as very difficult to perform easily, and since most Americans are not familiar with the Korean culture, martial arts is beneficial as a practical application on how to apply correct kinesiology to daily working activities.

I have treated ADHD students with simple forms. If the students' progress, I gradually use more advanced forms as moving meditations.

Excerpts from Other Books by Myung Chill Kim

Books are available for purchase on Amazon.com

Tae Kwon Do

Kwang Moo Ryu Style
Kinesiology of Martial Arts

Volume I: Essentials

Fifth Revision

Myung Chill Kim

Kinesiology for Martial Artists and Athletes of the 21st Century

The study of Kinesiology does not align with martial arts movements modernized over the last 100 years.

Master Myung Chill Kim has combined theories of Tae Kwon Do, Karate, Shaolin and Praying Mantis style Kung Fu and Boxing to:

- Correct the profound loss of historical peak efficiency, with CHANGE which must come to the Basics, Forms, Breaking, Sparring and Fighting Techniques.

- Learn how to paralyze an opponent with Praying Mantis and Kicking techniques.

- Learn how to practice with a patented Isokinetic Resistance Pad.

- Reveal the secret of Maximum force using ankle and wrist weights to rebalance and strengthen the form's dynamics.

- Cast the VIBRATING PALM (Iron Palm) with this training method.

8.5" x 11" 300 pages, 353 illustrations
Visit www.TKDBOOK.COM for more information

Myung Chill Kim
1965 - Korean Tiger Troops TKD instructor (Vietnam War)
1981 - Criminal Investigator for New York City Dept. of Ports.
1986 – Degree of Doctor of Oriental Medicine

Author of:
1971 - "Acupuncture for Self Defense"
1997 - "Oriental Medicine and Cancer"
1999 - "Chi Gong: Medicine from God"
2009 - "Tae Kwon Do (Kwang Moo Ryu)"

$39.95
ISBN 978-0-9970399-7-9
53995>

AVAILABLE SPRING 2023:

TAE KWON DO (KWANG MOO RYU) 5th Edition

If someone teaches ballet, the movement is standard all over the world. However, Tae Kwon Do Karate kicks are done differently by each person. We need a standard movement with kinesiology.

What is the correct side kick? What is the standard side kick?

A side kick should have both arms moving in opposite directions during the kick. This correct side kick posture results in the most powerful side kick, plus if the opponent is blocking or pushing, the side kick posture balance will be sustained with proper kinesiology.

Sidekicks with Tae Kwon Do and Karate use two hands holding in front of the chest while kicking. Some martial artists incorrectly think two hands held onto the chest pose is better than both hands stretching sideways, as in the figure below.

Unfortunately, the hands can only be used to punch after the foot lands on the ground. From the kicking pose, bring hands together, land the foot first, then punch. Whether the hands are stretched or together while kicking does not make a big difference.

178

These photos are in the Tae Kwon Do textbook.
You can see the Tae Kwon Do videos on
www.kwangmooryu.com. If you want to learn the
correct way of martial arts, subscribe to my Kwang
Moo Ryu videos.

Above is an incorrect jumping sidekick in most Tae Kwon Do and Karate textbooks. This kick looks like an airplane with two wings on one side.

Even when you kick the air, even when you hit the target, or especially when the opponent blocks you, you will have a crash landing on the ground.

Above is the correct jumping side kick.
This perfect balance of the jumping side kick kinesiology using the right hand and left-hand balance pushing in opposite directions, is correct.

This is the correct position for the jumping side kick, even when you kick the air, even when you hit the target, or even when the opponent blocks you, you can have a safe landing.

Roundhouse kick

www.kwangmooryu.com

The correct kinesiology for the roundhouse kick technique is as follows: swing arms and turn the waist before the kick to create two to three times more powerful force than the ordinary Tae Kwon Do or Karate kick. This kinesiology technique also prevents injuries. Watch accuracy of martial art movements

The watermelon video is different than in the photo. The watermelon in the video has a spear holding the round, very hard watermelon that resembles a basketball. Master Kim was able to slice the watermelon one inch from the spearhead.

Master Myung Chill Kim is demonstrating speed and accuracy by cutting a watermelon with a razor-sharp samurai sword on a student's stomach with his eyes closed.

Without the sense of sight, one of the five senses, Master Kim can conquer the sixth sense of slicing a watermelon with no sight.

The watermelon depicted above in the video is a hard, round watermelon that was available in the late fall season in the Boston, Massachusetts area.

Please watch my health and Martial Art demonstration videos at www.kwangmooryu.com. I have twenty-one videos, but I have finished uploading only nine videos on my website. The videos contain twenty-one correct Tae Kwon Do forms (Japanese call this form "kata").

Most of the "breaking demonstration" movements, even using a stationary object, are incorrect in both form and style. See the Tae Kwon Do textbook.

Forms

Tae Kwon Do and Karate practitioners are good in sparring, but the forms (*kata*) do not have much connected movements. If they are engaged in real fighting situations, they can fight as they are practicing sparring in a school. But if they were to be sucker punched or kicked first, they would be at a major disadvantage.

Kung Fu forms have more connected movements than Tae Kwon Do and Karate forms, but there are not enough sparring techniques for it to be useful in real situations.

Shadow Boxing movements are very useful in real fighting situations, even if you suddenly get hit first by an opponent and you can still use continuous movements.

Most of Kwang Moo Ru's forms were designed for continuous movement in practical applications. It has the best martial arts forms for the 21st century with correct kinesiology and connected movements.

Bruce Lee passed away in 1973. Lee learned Tae Kwon Do kicks from a Korean master in Oklahoma City, Oklahoma, and from another master in Washington, D.C. around the late 1960s. Unfortunately, Lee's masters were unable to teach him the correct kinesiology of kicking.

Lee practiced Tae Kwon Do kicks for many hours per day, including roundhouse and back spinning kick combinations. He severely injured his lower back and had spinal surgery.

The surgeon advised Lee that he should not practice any more kicks for the rest of his life. Once he reached world fame, many movie roles were rushed onto Lee. When he shot movies in Asia, Lee used a Korean Tae Kwon Do black belt as his stunt double because he had too much pain and had to use steroids and endo-opioids to ease back pain.

Therefore, non-kinesiology-based movements of hands and feet maneuvers will injure martial artists and shorten their lifespans. Survey shows that the average life span of martial artists are 70 years of age.

The correct application of kinesiology in martial arts to scenes of UFC full contact matches might be changed. However, because Master Kim's martial art techniques are very powerful and dangerous, Master Kim is concerned that these techniques will permanently injure or kill the opponents, even in UFC fighting sports arenas. Real martial artists cannot play with these serious techniques. If martial artists apply this kinesiology of Martial Art techniques, then more serious injuries will occur.

THE LAST 120 YEARS HAS BEEN THE DARK AGES OF MARTIAL ARTS.

WE SHOULD PRACTICE CORRECT KINESIOLOGY FOR PRESENT AND FUTURE GENERATIONS.

CHI GONG

MEDICINE FROM GOD

3RD EDITION

MYUNG CHILL KIM

STRENGTHEN YOUR BODY AND CALM YOUR MIND WITH CHI GONG BREATHING EXERCISES

A third of Americans have been treated with Acupuncture, but few have felt *Chi* energy or knowledge of Chi Gong.

Chi energy is built through internal martial art styles such as slow breathing exercises, meditation, and fasting.

Chi Gong helps the body attain longevity and health, improve energy circulation, balance mood and mental health, treat Coronavirus, and more.

3rd Edition includes:
- More information on Korean Chi Gong
- More physical Chi Gong exercises
- Updated instructions on how to deliver baby easily
- Dangers of practicing Chi Gong improperly and imposter practitioners
- New and improved illustrations

For helpful videos, please visit www.youtube.com/@myungchillkim

6" x 9"
247 Pages
$19.95 USD

E-book available for the
first time on amazon.com

Fig. 3-47

Sending Chi energy is not easily understood by ordinary people. It works differently as in a different dimension. It will not only penetrate a wall but, it can also transmit through many walls and at any distance. (Fig. 3-47)

I can demonstrate this to a group of students while I am standing three walls away from the students and sending Chi energy thru walls. A witness standing in the middle of us on the corridor can observe when I send Chi energy thru the wall. Close-eyed students respond by moving their hand. Sometimes I demonstrate through other connected stores in the same building with 20 walls.

Fig. 3-48

Fig. 3-49

I can send Chi energy a long distance and this has been witnessed by telephone. It is not Chi sending through the telephone. A witness person answers the phone and hears my sound when I send Chi to the receiving person with closed eyes and responds to it by moving the fingers. The witness could be in a different room and feel the chi energy. The success rate is 90 percent. (Fig.3-48) (Fig.3-49)

I did it from Oklahoma City, Oklahoma to Boston, Massachusetts. This is 1,750 miles. It works in different dimensions. It works by your noble intention. Your will power can move Chi energy to any-where in the Universe.

A Tae Kwon Do master, who was also a dedicated Chi Gong practitioner since the age of 65 years old, used to do pushups one thousand times per day until 80 years old.

The master had heart attack and passed away 6 years later. The master did not learn the art of Chi Gong practice correctly, which resulted in death.

An acclaimed World Korean Chi Gong Organization founder in Arizona trained a 35-year-old lady from New York City in the middle of a hot summer. The Chi Gong master asked the woman to climb the hill with 30 pounds of weight in a backpack.
The woman died from a heart attack while climbing.

There is a correct way and an incorrect way to teach about the separate internal and external nature of the Chi Gong martial arts.

Even in historical religious texts, there are fundamental principles about the Creation of

Life from the beginning of the book. Sun Tzu wrote The Art of War with basic war principles as a fundamental instruction.

Similarly, Chi Gong has fundamental principles about internal and external nature in martial arts.

In the tragic examples about the Chi Gong so-called "masters" who ended up harming themselves and others, the masters clearly did not know very basic principles of internal and external nature in martial arts.

So, do not mix both internal and external styles of Martial Art. In other words, heavy weightlifting and /or strenuous physical exercise (external style) and Chi Gong (internal style) should not be mixed.

ORIENTAL MEDICINE AND CANCER

Revised Edition

MYUNG CHILL KIM

193

1. Myung Kim's Four Inter Channel Theory is introduced in this book, which includes:

    - Gall Bladder problem (hip joint) causes tumors or cancers in the ovary, uterus, breast, testicle, prostate, and brain.

    - Treat people with acupuncture needles with Chi energy infusion.

    - I specialize in treating breast tumors with Chi energy.

2. For the first time in TCM history, Myung Kim's Diagonal Symmetry Points Acupuncture

3. Specialize in treating infertility, breached birth, and delayed birth.

    - ✓ Pregnant women will benefit from Chi infusion with or without needles once or twice per month.

    - ✓ After the baby is born, the new mother will recover much faster, her baby will be born with extra Chi energy, and the baby will be more energetic than other babies.

4. Athletes can get Chi energy from me and their athletic performance will improve and may break world record

5. Cancer is caused by external injuries that block the Chi energy flow channels too.

> ✓ Spinal injuries and surgery scars can cause cancer.

6. The American government has spent over 50 billion dollars for cancer research since the 1970s Nixon Administration, yet still has not found the cure for many cancers.

7. Western medicine and science will never figure it or understand the cause of cancer without my help (Oriental medicine)

In 1999, a Jewish doctor who is one of my martial art acquaintances introduce me two young Chinese doctors. They tried to survey my theory that spinal injury and hip joint problem to cause cancers on reproductive organ and brain.

They asked the patients record of who had spinal injury or surgery in hospitals in Boston, Massachusetts area but all of them refused to cooperate.

Any medical organization or any country want to learn and/or research my theory please contact me:

info@myungchillkim.com

Introduction:

"Gentlemen and Ladies"

"I have traveled around the Eastern, Western, Southern, and Northern parts of the United States."

To understand Oriental Medicine, Westerners must open their minds to the vast differences between Eastern and Western ways of thinking. There are profound differences in orientation, approaches to movement, ways in which language is used to refer to movement in nature, and the perception of how human beings are related to nature.

People in American, European, Arabic, and Indian cultures think about direction in the following sequence: North, South, East, and West (four directions). Western culture is characterized by movement and exploration.

The sailing of ships in search of new lands and new opportunities for trade, and the voyages through space in pursuit of knowledge about the universe — these restless movements of the Western mind are perhaps guided using the Northern star as a point of orientation.

In Taoist terms, we would say that as a culture of movement, the West is Yang.

In Eastern culture, in contrast, Chinese and Korean people orient according to:

East, West, South, and North. People have been tempered by thousands of years of agriculture. The orientation towards life and health is based on farming, literally cultivating "what is." Relative to the West, we could be called a Yin culture.

When Koreans sleep, they point their heads towards the East or South. As you will learn in this book, Chi Gong and other forms of meditation also recommend facing East and South. The rising of the sun and its heating of the earth influenced the livelihood of our ancestors so much that we still use it as a basis for orienting our lives.

The Chinese, Mongols, and Tibetans have basic directional orientations that they use in daily living. In China, the dead are displayed in their houses during mourning in coffins with their heads facing north or the deceased is buried facing north underground; this tradition has been adopted by Koreans. Mongols, like Koreans, build their houses facing South to take advantage of the sun's light and heat since their weather can be extremely cold.

Another example illustrating the differences in orientation between the West and the East is the compass. The Chinese originally invented the magnetic compass, called the Chi Nan Jen - Chi meaning pointing; Nan meaning South and Jen meaning needle. Westerns assumed, when they recreated the compass for their use, that the magnetic direction was north. Once again, we see the clear-cut difference in orientation.

Traditional Chinese Medicine and Contemporary American Society

The lifestyle of a Chinese farmer has not changed dramatically over the past thousand years. There have been some technological advances and certainly there is better access to health care, but the basic conditions of life and work are similar.

Thus, the health problems described in the medical classics closely resemble those faced by a contemporary doctor of Traditional Chinese Medicine. However, if this Asian doctor were to come to the United States to speak, the doctor might find that the lecture did not fit as well with the contemporary American situation.

Today in the United States We See:

•More mental stress

•Labor involving machinery

•Auto accident-related injuries

•Gunshot wounds

•Sports addiction (Over-exercise)

•Emotional trauma resulting from broken family life, abuse, etc.

•Damage to the ear, including partial loss of hearing, due to vibrations from loud music

•Surgical scarring

•Cancer

•Drug problems

•Heavy emphasis on competition on the job, in sports, etc.

•Dietary problems like anorexia, bulimia, and resulting malnutrition

•Bodily harm from popular, dangerous sports such as sky diving, rock climbing, parachuting, bungee jumping, white water rafting, race car driving, football, boxing, kick boxing and full contact martial art matches.

These modern American health problems are not directly discussed in the Chinese medical classics and require modern approaches. Since the United States is a nation with lifestyles, cultures, and dietary habits radically different from those of China, the practice of Oriental Medicine in the United States must necessarily diverge somewhat from that practiced in China today.

But Oriental Medicine can be adapted for people who live in modern industrialized countries. This book has been written to show how different Oriental medical theories can fit the health problems that plague Americans at the end of the Twentieth Century and into the Twenty First Century.

Excerpt from Chapter 11 - Cancer and Oriental Medicine:

I remember that when I first came to the U.S. in 1970, I was surprised to see how American children built their snowmen. As you know, an American snowman usually has three parts: a large base, a smaller trunk, and a still smaller head. In Asia, we built snowmen in two parts: a head and a body.

Most of Caucasian Americans are much taller than the average Asian. This additional height leads to more strain on the neck and lower back, as well as more susceptibility to injury in those areas. In addition, Caucasian Americans are more prone to osteoporosis as they age than are Asians because of the additional stress on their bones. In light of these facts, it is interesting that the American snowman is divided both at the neck and the lower trunk/back, while the Asian snowman is not.

In my practice, I have found that taller people without any spinal or physical injuries get breast cancer, Hodgkin's lymphoma – cancer of the lymphatic system. I suspect that taller people with Norwegian, Finnish, Swedish (Scandinavian countries) are more susceptible to varicose veins because blood and lymph fluids are not able to reach the brain and upper part of the body easily.

Therefore, taller people are more susceptible to lymphoma and cancer. Shorter people, such as the French, are not necessarily susceptible to the same group of diseases as taller people. Usually, shorter people live longer than taller people.

Fig. 6 - 5

"BA GUA" = (equals)

Three Dimension Ba Gua System

About 3000 B.C.E., the legendary figure Fuxi is said to have lived in China. He is credited with developing the Ba Gua (eight trigrams) and writing the I-Ching (64 hexa grams).

Original Ba Gua symbol: Who designed this? How long ago? No one knows.

In China, the Chinese interpret Ba Gua symbol as Two-Dimensional. North, South, East, West, Northeast, Northwest, Southeast, Southwest (8 directions).

I am the first person in thousands of years who interpret Ba Gua as three-dimensional. I think I am the author who understood the original mind of the Ba Gua creator.

My book has the Western Cartesian Coordination System in Eastern Yin/Yang Theory (See also page 67 in the First Edition of the Oriental Medicine and Cancer book, published in 1996.

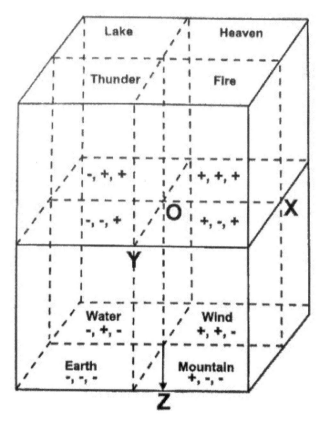

Three Dimension Ba Gua System

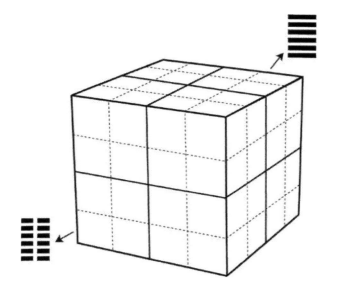

Fig. 6-12

This famous I-Ching system is usually used for fortune-telling using a six-hexagram system. I converted this I-Ching system as a four-story building with sixty-four rooms. Each room of the original eight room building is divided into eight, leaving sixty-four rooms.

Kinesiology:
Common Sense II
Coming Soon

- Simple and Innovative Physical Therapy Techniques

- Never before seen techniques and physical exercises for neck, shoulder, elbow, wrist, lower back, hip, knee, ankle, and joint pain

- Emergency Acupressure for Fainting and Fever

- How to Treat Heart Palpitation and Panic Attack

- How to Treat Indigestion and Gastro spasm

- How to Control Sea Sickness and Nausea

- How to Treat Vertigo and Dizziness

- How to Treat Gallstone Pain

- How to Control Severe Kidney Stone Pain

- How to Treat Toothache

EACH MONTH, I WILL PUBLISH A

Martial Arts Newsletter

WITH AN ARTICLE AND PHOTO AND/OR
VIDEO FOR FREE ONLY AT:

WWW.KWANGMOORYU.COM

Tai Chi Yu ™

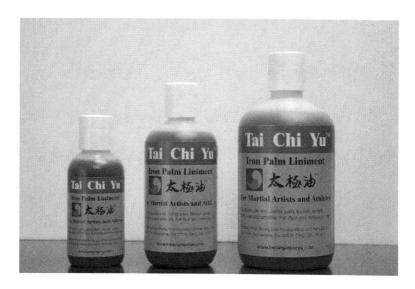

4 oz.   **8 oz**   **16 oz.**

The above photos of **Tai Chi Yu™ ("iron palm liniment")** contains **Dit Da Jow™** original formula plus very secret family ingredients dissolved in water and glycerin. Tai Chi Yu™ is great for iron palm training, joint pain, arthritis, ingrown hairs, bruises, psoriasis, itchiness, body odor and minor cuts.

TAI CHI YU ORDER FORM

Please allow 1 to 2 weeks for delivery

[ ] Tai Chi Yu   4 oz Bottle $19.95 ea

[ ] Tai Chi Yu   8 oz Bottle $34.95 ea

[ ] Tai Chi Yu   16 oz Bottle $59.95 ea

ADD $8.95 for S&H per item: **+ $8.95**

OKLAHOMA Residents MUST ADD 8.625% TAX

WE ACCEPT PAYMENT VIA PAYPAL ONLY.

Email this form invoice and send payment to:

ordersmyungckim@gmail.com

SHIPPING ADDRESS

Name:

Address:

City:

State:

Zip:

Email:

Made in the USA
Columbia, SC
10 February 2023

11883362R00117